Blessings
AND INCLEMENCIES

Blessings
AND INCLEMENCIES
poems

CONSTANCE MERRITT

LOUISIANA STATE UNIVERSITY PRESS

BATON ROUGE

Published by Louisiana State University Press
Copyright © 2007 by Constance Merritt
All rights reserved
An LSU Press Paperback Original
Manufactured in the United States of America
First printing

Designer: Barbara Neely Bourgoyne
Typeface: Whitman
Printer and binder: Thomson-Shore, Inc.

Grateful acknowledgment is made to the editors of the following periodicals, in which the poems listed first appeared: "Among Shades: VII," *Harvard Review* (Spring 2002); "Turning," *The Journal* (Spring 2000); "Morning Song," "The Weighing," *Lyric Poetry Review* (Winter/Spring 2004); "Waking," *Malahat Review* (Winter 1998); "Faces," reprinted from *Prairie Schooner* 79:3 (Fall 2005), copyright University of Nebraska Press, 2005; "Song: At the Edge of the Sea," reprinted from *Prairie Schooner* 73:1 (Spring 1999), copyright University of Nebraska Press, 1999; "The Unconsoled," reprinted from *Prairie Schooner* 79:2 (Summer 2005), copyright University of Nebraska Press, 2005; "Daily Office," "Lines for the Cartographer, Lost," *Radcliffe Quarterly* (Fall 2001); "Three O'Clock," *Ragged Edge* premiere issue (January/February 1997); "Dwelling," *Ragged Edge* (January 2001); "2 A.M.: The Body as Weaver," "6 A.M.: Meditation: Entering the Mind of Winter," "Coda," *Ragged Edge* (May 2001); "Spring," *Women's Review of Books* (May 1998).

Lines from "The Blue Swallows" by Howard Nemerov are reprinted courtesy of Margaret Nemerov. Lines from "Lacunae" by Hilda Raz in "Rising" are reprinted courtesy of Hilda Raz. Lines from *Orlando* by Virginia Woolf in "Idyll" are reprinted courtesy of the Society of Authors as the literary representative of the estate of Virginia Woolf. Copyright 1928 by Virginia Woolf and renewed 1956 by Leonard Woolf, reprinted by permission of Harcourt, Inc. "Open House," copyright 1941 by Theodore Roethke, "A Walk in Late Summer," copyright 1957 by Theodore Roethke, from *The Collected Poems of Theodore Roethke* by Theodore Roethke. Used by permission of Doubleday, a division of Random House, Inc., and Faber and Faber Ltd. Lines from "Autumn Day" by Rainer Maria Rilke are copyright 1982 by Stephen Mitchell, from *The Selected Poetry of Rainer Maria Rilke* by Rainer Maria Rilke, translated by Stephen Mitchell. Used by permission of Random House, Inc. Excerpt from "A Man Meets a Woman in the Street" from *The Complete Poems* by Randall Jarrell. Copyright 1969, renewed 1997 by Mary von S. Jarrell. Reprinted by permission of Farrar, Straus and Giroux, LLC, and Faber and Faber Ltd.

Library of Congress Cataloging-in-Publication Data
Merritt, Constance, 1966–
    Blessings and inclemencies : poems / Constance Merritt.
        p. cm.
    ISBN-13: 978-0-8071-3258-6 (pbk. : alk. paper)
    I. Title
    PS3563.E74536B64 2007
    811'.54—dc22

                                                                    2006102803

The paper in this book meets the guidelines for permanence and durability of the Committee on Production Guidelines for Book Longevity of the Council on Library Resources. ∞

for Eleanor Wilner—chief
among blessings

and

for A. R. Ammons
in memoriam

O swallows, swallows, poems are not
The point. Finding again the world,
That is the point, where loveliness
Adorns intelligible things
Because the mind's eye lit the sun.

—HOWARD NEMEROV, "The Blue Swallows"

Contents

Song
AT THE EDGE OF THE SEA

after Rachel L. Carson

I

In a world where the hands go hungry, where
Daily the tongues of men murder even
The sturdiest hearts; where the old gods are fallen
And the soul subsists on facts; in a world where
Frenzied, ceaseless racket harries the ear
And one by one the instruments are broken,
Never to be restrung, their songs forgotten;
Where wisdom speaks in tones we cannot hear . . .

In a world where neither distance is nor rest,
Where is comfort? Where is nearness? East
Of evil? West of regret? Will there be words
To tell the stones what ails us? Stones . . . a world?
Who will tell us the names of stars
Or till the earth to plant our tears?

II

The world is complete without us. Intolerable fact.
A fact, indeed, but not intolerable.
I've seen the world without us and it lacked
Nothing, but burned on fierce and beautiful.
Or should I say it lacked all things
Human: malice, injustice, garbage, greed.

The nuclear winters, the silent springs
Of our machinations slowly fade
With our dark souls into oblivion;
The body of the animal alone
Remains, open to the vast pavilion
Of sky, gathered in at last, at rest, at one.
There is life without us; there is song.
We learn to sing that we too might belong.

III

For there is life without us; let us then praise
Protophyta and protozoa: blue-green
Algae, yellow-green, and life that falls between
The system's cracks—both plant and animal in its ways;
The dinoflagellates, their smoldering blaze
Reddening the tides. Thallophyta: green
And red and brown algae—sargassum weed,
Dulse, Irish moss, and kelp. And spare no praise
For Porifera, the sponge; Coelenterata:
Jellyfish, corals, hydroids, anemones—
Their stinging cells impaling passing prey.
The translucent comb jellies, Ctenophora;
And the flatworms, Platyhelminthes,
Whose cells occur in three primary layers.

IV

Unstinting praise for festive ribbon worms—
Their extreme shyness and stark autonomy;
For bristle worms; and for the five-classed and many-
Specied Arthropoda, whose diverse forms
(The jointed foot be praised!) walk, swim, squirm,
Make sense of their environs, handle prey—
Among them: lobster, shrimp, and crab; the highly
Phosphorescent ostracods. Here beasts and terms
Abound: spiders, king crab, mites, and centipedes . . .
Bryozoa: moss animals and sea laces;
Echinodermata's multiples of five:
Starfish, sea urchins, brittle stars. The soft
Armored bodies of mollusks; sea squirts. The race is
Not ours to forfeit or to win. We've
Barely landed and lie gasping in the weeds;
We cannot see or hold our heads aloft.

V

As we drowse upon the nipple of the earth—
The sea still in our ears, salt on our breath—
We learn to sing that we too might belong,
Making of mother's milk a gurgle song;
But not to sound the depths of our pure mirth
Or tell the soundless terrors of our birth.
Nor do we sing to mourn the body wrung
From that wet world. The stars, the moon are hung
So far above us, likewise the face we long
So desperately to touch—now and always.
Our arms can reach so far; the world eludes
Us. Finding scant comfort in the distant gaze,
We fling ourselves into the world on floods
Of sound, or draw it near to us with siren song.

VI

We set much store by meaning, but I suspect
It's academic, an elaborate evasion
Of some widely known and well-hidden fact
Which if recognized just might occasion
A reappraisal of the human,
Its relation to the animal. Tool use,
Language, suicide, an exile and dominion
Divinely planned: thus we will excuse
Ourselves from life on earth. Yet how can we
Be sure this noise we make is human, is
Not deeply rooted in the beast? Maybe
These words are just baroque versions of bark and hiss.
I hate you sung in soothing tones will lull
The child, and sense does not make birdsong beautiful.

VII

We heard someone say Sirens so we came
Once more to set the twisted record straight
Should there be one who'll hear our side of it:
We had no dark designs; song was our aim.
What use had we for foolish men? Or fame?
The sea's no place for children, yet we wept
To see them dashed upon our rocks. They leapt,
Gods don't know why, so we kept watch to claim
Them from the soup. At first we sang to warn
Them from our rocks. The ships took heed, and yet
Each crossing left a mess of sodden men.
And so it was we came at last to learn
To weave with our voices the subtlest nets
To catch the stars, bright fish, mercurial men.

VIII

So you see, there were nets, a song's a net;
It hauls you out of Time, out of whatever
Broth you're stewing in. Question's whether
You'll be hauled. So many couldn't let
Go of their stern wills long enough to let
Us save their lives. Safe under no shelter,
They'd sooner drown than ride the waves, would rather
Be themselves than be alive. All true, and yet
Some gave themselves fully to sea and net,
Falling as ripe fruit falls—not surrender,
But prayer, a winnowing, a rapture.
And in that moment, of course, they did forget,
But forgetting is not death; they got it wrong;
Those who listened lived in being's song.

IX

But wait! Without us who would name the world?
And isn't it the naming that we love
And not the thing itself? We don't want *bird*,
But *starling, osprey, titmouse, crow,* and *dove.*
The naturalist may well be a de facto poet,
But how often does it work the other way
Around?
          After reading, I dream of *bluet*
And *stylet*—not the things, but words (who knows why).
Another time, I drown my five year old
Niece in the bath, but she survives, becomes
An eel. Falling from great heights we take hold
Of what's at hand.
          I parse the peaceable kingdoms,
Wedding words to lives, holding neither cheap,
Until, at last, dumb with fatigue, I sleep.

X

Does the crow say *crow* or *constance* or something else?
Addressed, I look up with quickening pulse.
Once it was not so easy for the world
To woo me; I needed trumpets and a herald
Of angels. Now, a single bird will do—
A pigeon or a crow. Shit happens; you
Die all at once or bit by bit or change,—
Nothing so ponderous as your life—arrange
The smallest gestures in the key of light,
Read what before you'd never read, write
Instead of phone. Once, a mere girl,
I imagined I possessed the fabled pearl
Of great price; speaking, I found my voice
Natural, my tongue uncleft as yet by knowledge, choice.

XI

How dull we are at birth, toothless and whole,
A haft without a tool, a bladeless knife,
A cul-de-sac, an O without a hole,
But late or soon we drink the brine of life:
We're drawn along the whetstone of the world;
We're clothed in taut horsehairs, seasoned with rosin,
Or abandoned in a quiver; we're whirled
Until we grab onto this spinning rock like lichen.
Sharpened, seasoned, softened—it never stops.
Whosever kitchen this is we've stumbled into,
The cook's meticulous—seven dollops
Of gall for one of thyme. What does one do?
Choice isn't wide: bend or break, curse or bleat,
Refuse the dance or dance, die and eat.

XII

Refuse the dance or dance. We hesitate,
Lean far out of our bodies listening.
The tune is unfamiliar, the rhythm complicated;
We fret like newborns at a christening.
Meanwhile the spendthrift world is glistening—
Every limb and leaf. The din will lure
Us yet.
           It's late. Dawn is hastening.
One by one, we leave the walls, move out onto the floor.
What happens after that we can't be sure,
Although, as always, speculation's rife:
Each dry stick takes root, becomes a flower;
We study war no more; Love lies with Strife . . .
Me, I'd like to think the rhythm moved
Us, until the dance, itself, was what we loved.

I

Requiem

for Mary Ann McCabe, 1954–1997

I. "One Is About to Leave, the Other Is Staying"

And does it really matter which is which?
Or if the sharp sweet music of departure
Reaches them or dies away on wind,
    Their eyes unopened?

II. Idyll

It was always summer then and afternoon;
The leaves rustled like laughter in the trees,
Like laughter that young girls staying up late—
Their bodies tense and close till mirth subside—
Would press deep into pillows like a kiss
Lest sober elders hear and come to chide.

Day after day at half past noon they'd meet
In the long schoolroom to learn mythology—

     How when the last great war in heaven was won
     The mighty victor Jove (called *Zeus* by Greeks)
     Took ambrosia and broke with vanquished foes,
     And took their goddesses to him to wife,
     Hoping to found one kingdom with his blood
     (Called *ichor* coursing through the veins of gods);

     How Styx alone remained recalcitrant,
     Unwilling to submit her will to his;
     She would remain a force to reckon with,
     A name even those haughty gods would dread;
     And so it was gods came to swear by Styx
     And suffer exile should such vow be broken;

     How one there rose who seeing gods new fallen
     Into the ways of decadence and greed—
     Indifferent, unkind to care-worn men—
     Would match his wits against the mind of Jove
     And win for them the better part of kine
     And warm the dank cold mindcave with quick fire;

     How golden days hardened to bronze, to iron.
     How keeping flocks or bathing by the shore
     The green daughters of men were ravished by

The many-minded one and left to fly,
Harried by cow-eyed Hera's jealousy—
The wanderings of Io, Leda's life

Split open by the knowledge of a god;
Niobe brought to grief by mother's pride.
How, picking flowers in far fields of youth,
Demeter's only darling, Persephone,
Not even she, not even she was spared,
But shuddering knew the first foretaste of death;

How, obstinate in grief, Demeter wept,
Sealed up her great earthwomb, turned blood to stone
So nothing grew till Death gave back her daughter
(For only half the year, utterly changed).
How Dionysus, god of wine and song,
Sued Death for his dam, Semele, and won;

How Orpheus won Eurydyce through song,
But failed by fault of tenderness to rise
From that dark world, his halting bride in tow,
And losing her again himself was lost
In ceaseless wanderings and in the eyes,
Some deep and swarthy, others deep and clear,

Of foreign boys. His lovely severed limbs.
His singing head. How Aesculapius,
Apollo's son, star pupil of wise Chiron,
Had skill to raise the dead until Zeus slew him;
And rash Antigone buried alive
Rather than live with men's hubris and lies—

And lessons done they'd walk into the world—
Still shivering (the room was always cold),
Still innocent of everything they'd read,
Laughing, so glad to feel the sun—the one,

Face open to the world, as it were sun,
The other one cast down as if ashamed,
Afraid of the vast world and what she was;
One touch-me-not, the other nootka rose.
How casually the two revealed themselves,
Haunting the aisles of record stores as once

Girls lingered languidly at pasture gates
To listen to the songs that shepherds sang.
And the world was young again, all things *that* new.
They walk, the one keeping the rhythm and
Their bearings with her cane, the other following,
Blind to everything except this face.

And what they say is what all lovers say,
All friends, entranced by possibility
Of what they might become, transfigured by
Another pair of eyes, how skins might shine
Like beaten gold and feel as soft as cashmere,
Well burnished by another pair of hands.

So what they say is what all lovers say
(Though they will not have time to lose their shyness):

> And then, *wrapped in their sables, they would talk*
> (*Sables,* because Nebraska nights turn cold
> Or else they did in long-forgotten times
> Of which we speak) *of everything under*
> *The sun; of sights and travels; of moors and pagans;*
> *Of this man's beard and that woman's skin;*
>
> *Of a rat that fed from her hand at table;*
> *Of the arras that moved always in the hall*
> *At home; of a face; of a feather. Nothing was*
> *Too small for such converse, nothing was too great.*

It was always summer then and afternoon;
The leaves rustled like laughter in the trees,
Like laughter that young girls staying up late—
Their bodies tense and close till mirth subside—
Would press deep into pillows like a kiss
Lest sober elders hear and come to chide.

And it was summer then and afternoon.
And so they walked and walked and talked and talked,
Parted and met, parted and met again;
And every time they met they were amazed,
As if a second sun had graced the sky,
As if they'd heard the music of the spheres.

III. Lines for the Cartographer, Lost

Nightly in your prayers remember the late cartographer, lost
In his long labors to raise the continent of absence.

Remember years of loneliness and dogged refusal
To relinquish a self-imposed task that was clearly futile:

To number and name innumerable countries, christening each
With shape and shade, intent upon intimate knowledge of terrain.

Remember his fierce fidelity beyond the bend in the road,
The subtle rise that revealed the land's betrayal. Let come what may

He'd trace the treacherous waters from tributaries to source,
Clothe each aching silence with a voice, and burnish the granite hills

Into terraces of undulant flesh, where, given time
And cherishing in the cartographer's fecund mind,

The beloved's vanished face might one day grow—live oak, sunflower,
   wild rose

IV. The Unconsoled

That bloodcurdling cry, that sharp ascending wail:
Wooooh sweet jesus somebody wake up the world!
Adrenaline still courses through my veins
And I am running banging on my own front door
To rouse my father slow to rouse inside;
When the 911 woman asks if he's alive
I tell her *I don't know his wife just found*
Him please god you've got to send someone!

After the coroner has come and shown
How purple marks on the dead man's chest spell *heart*
Attack, pronounced him dead, zipped up the bag
And gone, She, the girl I was, stands out
Behind her neighbor's pulpwood truck—the truck
He did not drive today, nor will drive
Tomorrow or tomorrow or the next day—
Alone but for the moon whose unaccountable
Countenance she abhors. She sets out the
Equation in her head: on one side,
This moon and the gold light of an ordinary day
In southern autumn, the smell of burning leaves
Sharp on the air of early afternoon;
On the other, this man, their neighbor, her father's
Bosom friend, husband, father, grandfather,
Hammer in hand about some routine labor,
Falling among the litter of leaves in his own
Backyard and lying there as light etched
The hours on the trees—mid-morning, noon;
First sun then moon.
                        She frowns hard as she worries
The equation. And then the dead man's wife is at
Her side, saying, *Hon, don't take it so to heart;*
Come back inside where it's warm with the rest of us.
Perhaps she feels how cold and still the girl is,
Feels it inside herself and dares not touch her

Lest, in steering the other back to life,
Her strength should fail and the girl should pull her over.
On one side, the girl is thinking while they wait,
The whole of life, this world, my own small life,
Frail cargo of not quite eighteen years;
And on the other, Michelle, at twenty,
Murdered, Helen murdered at forty-nine,
Tammy, like herself, not quite eighteen, nine
Months dead from cancer.
                              Let others justify
The ways of God to men; she never would.
She'd already stood the s.o.b. on trial,
Stood life itself on trial and found both
Wanting.
                  But who was she to keep a grieving
Woman shivering in cold? And so she moved
As if to say that *yes*, she would come in,
Although inside she knew she never would.

V. In Time

In time, of course, she'd learn to bear her dead,
Not with ease, but well enough to stand
And make her way carefully through the world.

She'd hold them to her breast as they were flowers,
Or babes she would not bear, and there they'd nestle,
Weighing almost nothing, a warmth, a pressure . . .

What weighed most was her own obdurate life.
Somehow it shamed her. How had she been spared?
Long nights she burned with guilt, ingratitude.

But also with the passion to be good,
Not worthier than they, but worthy still . . .
To redeem her life some day or else to kill

What could not be redeemed. Except how rob
Them of the second life they lived in her,
And how to make the living understand.

More haltingly, she learned to bear her life,
And from a distance found she loved the world
· Though sometimes still she dreamed her death, the child,

Long hoped for, long awaited, and was calmed.
Still, all in all, she learned to bear her dead,
If not her life, with a modicum of ease.

At least until a new beloved was borne
From life, and she, once more, would have to bend
To take the body up, make room, straighten,

Balance, begin, once more, carefully, to walk.
Slight as they were, her dead would jostle then;
They would begin to weigh until she felt

Her chest cave in, her mind useless and numb
Like a foot that's gone to sleep. No, worse than that,
Irreparably frostbitten, sheer, dead loss.

VI. Her Hymn to Darkness

She thinks it's hawks she hears
Although it might be jays

She knows it's life she fears
Wanting the sheer ruin of days

The teeth of wind grown sharper
Night falling swifter harder

Staying longer
Till one hardly needs to rise

To light's occasion

꒰ꕤ꒱

Prophet of doom
High priestess of desolation

She plods through empty rooms
Shushing the lights droning hymns

What is the source of sadness?
The antidote to despair?

Life is the source of sadness
Or the smallness of the soul

Or the largeness it desires
Can't manage so despairs

And the antidote is deadly to the living

VII. Lacunae

Pages fall from the calendar.
Two weeks of cruel sunlight.
A body turning slowly

Into loam. The only light
The radio. For warmth
A woolen shawl. Rocking

All night in the rocking
Chair. Pulled up close
To the crackling fire,

The hypothetical fire
Of the radio. The hand
That seldom leaves the dial,

Intent on reeling in
A messenger from you—
To tell me   what?

Goodbye   hello
The singer of the one
Song I dream might hold . . .

Is it cruel that I
Can't care for any of their
Stories of where you are?

You are   not here. And even
As I remember you
From clues you left—the plum

I held up to your nose
When plums had come to seem
To us, absolved of eyes, so much

Like small ripe tomatoes—
I know that I am less,
In love, in gesture.

VIII. Roses

Your sister's voice is not your voice.
Your beloved's grace is not your grace.

I walked with him in a garden of roses.
He spoke their language, traced

Their complicated genealogies,
The vagaries of fragrance,

The rituals of care . . .

༺༻

Arms laden with long-stemmed roses, after
The school concert that I've come back to hear,

I walk backstage to where my music teacher—
A woman that I've known since I was five

And fiercely loved and feared since junior high—
Is laid out on the bed of strings, beneath

The upraised lid of her grand piano.
I cast the foolish, drooping, garish lids

Aside, and go to her, offering my hands;
Though frail, her pleas for talk and touch are fierce.

And then, solicitous, obliging her,
I feel the other's presence in the room,

The young man settled deep in shadow as if
A fixture there. He does not move or speak,

But softly clears his throat, meaning *you'll over
Tire her; it would be best if you would go.*

And in that moment's hesitation the dream
Frame shifts, repeats again, again, again—

Great-grandmother, grandmother, mother (Mom!),
Each imminently dying and interposed

Between us, inexorably, this shadow man.
And finally between my mom and me

A mound of toys the two of us must manage,
In the time before she dies, before there will

Be time for me or her, and I am on my knees
before the toys, facing her, beseeching,

To no avail. And then with such pure rage
And helplessness I am hurling hurling

Toys, one hand then the next, back, over my shoulders,
Eyes riveted to the figure that threatens to recede . . .

And so until I wake to pounding chest
And do not sleep again.

≈⌒≈

Meanwhile, this man, your husband—once,
Most intimate, though lately, most estranged—

Recites the names of roses,
Cups hybrid heads under the chin—

A gift, a solemn offering.
Dutifully, I bend rose after rose,

Though I don't want to know the things he knows,
Don't want to see the little stream

He wants to lead me to, down the steeply
Graded, dusk-secluded path

And will not go not even—
Especially—when he insists.

Stubbornly, he makes his slow way down
With aid of walking cane; stubbornly,

I grip the iron rail until the figure disappears.

And it is not the future I have dreamed;
Bitterly, bitterly, it is the past.

IX. Daily Office

Where does one begin
When the pale scent of autumn sadness tints
The air and the mind falls dim,

The fire in the mouthcave, ash?
Where does one begin and how and when?

Begin as best you can.

Begin in the chill of morning,
Slow calculus of loss etched into
Your soul with every breath;

Begin in summer fullness,
Curled foetus small, floating downstream in the frail
Wicker coracle of song;

And by the shore at sunset:
Enter the water, let the body drift
To where the hurt is deepest.

X. The Planting

I am beginning to forget, you said.
Once I held this city in my head,
Could find my way along its streets in sleep,
And tell a sighted person what was where;
But now the map is worn, the colors fading—
And since I lost my sight, of course, things change . . .
To lose my sight and then, the look of things . . .

To lose the look of things and then, the world . . .

꙼

A sunny day, vast field of stones:
We've come to lay the urn that holds
What's left of you to rest.
The Jehovah's witness murmurs
Some prayer I can't won't hear; they say
You'll sleep until the Savior comes
(They said you wanted this?)
And then shall rise to share, not heaven,
(It makes your sister wince)
But a lesser, earthly paradise.

꙼

I let you go, but I do not submit.
How dare they say, still feverish with life,
Still dizzy with the world, that you now sleep
In dust and it is best, for God knows best?
And me? For the sake of solacing my own
Dumb grief, what illusory fictions would I make?
I'd say, this world's a rack, a bed of nails
It's best to be turned out of soon than late,
But how with pulsing hand write *peace*, write *dust*
And count it good, the life you loved you lost?

I think what you were spared: renal failure,
Dialysis; better go quietly
In sleep some summer afternoon, a breeze
Lifting the curtains in your rooms, sweetening
The air, and as you drift, the whir of fans
And, far off, tidings from the world you love—
A car door slams, a woman laughs, snatches
Of melody, vaguely familiar, a drone,
A hymn, a lullaby; and now this new
Throbbing in the ear as another car grounds by,
Inexorable hip-hop beat mauling
The air. Slowly it dies away; you turn
And drift again, sink deeper into sleep . . .
And here am I while you are busy dying,
Still whirled inside the motions of my life
And powerless to help you had I known—No,
I'd read and I'd rehearsed it in my mind—
My fingers knuckle-deep inside the jar
Of honey (always there's honey in a house),
And then against the smooth, still warm, wet inside
Of your cheek, and while that slow sweetness travels
The length of throat, enters your blood, I'm on
The phone for help and then back at your side
Touching you as we've never touched before,
Making of words a ladder you can climb
Back up into your life, to me, this room;
I play it out like Ariadne's thread,
Return from where you've gone, I'm waiting here.
Don't go and leave me stranded on this shore.
But you can't hear because I am not there,
And where was I when you were busy dying?
O traveler, sweet warrior, loved friend . . .

Are you goin' to Scarborough Fair?—
    I hear their voices braiding in the wind,
Parsley, sage, rosemary, and thyme—

Your friends Hardy and Dave with their guitars,
Remember me to one who lives there,
Working the little garden where once we stirred,
She once was a true love of mine.
No music then except the birds' and yours.

Tell her to make me a ca'ambric shirt—
Though I do not approve I'd let you go,
Parsley, sage, rosemary, and thyme—
I'd let you go though I am not resigned,
Without no seam nor ne'edlework,
But love, the hour is late, where would you fly?
Then she'll be a true love of mine.
To unenchanted wood? To empty sky?—

Tell her to find me an acre of land—
This "You" who are a scattering of selves
Parsley, sage, rosemary, and thyme—
(Like every one of us, like every one)
Between the saltwater and the seastrand,
That held you near to them, that hold you still,
Then she'll be a true love of mine.
Fresh cutting planted deep within heart's rind.

II

Among Shades

A FRAGMENT

Unpitying, inexorable, but just;
a terrible, though not an evil, god.

—EDITH HAMILTON, *Mythology*

I

The war to end all wars, that's what we said,
To secure a life of harmony and ease—
What can I say? I was so young and stupid;
But is there one among you who'll say that these
Aren't noble virtues: harmony and ease,
Freedom from tyrants? Our grievances *were* valid.
They always are. Who can argue with Justice,
Mercy, Peace, Nostalgia for long-dreamed-of salad days?
The war to end all wars, that's what we said.
Now, I know that's what we'll always say—
Athena's owl flies only after dark. Aye . . .
Then, I knew only the heat of brothers
Closely huddled, conspiring together.
We rarely touched each other when we were freed.

II

The Titan gods against those born of Cronus
And the Hundred-Handed brought to light from darkness
(Brought from darkness into unnatural light
To expedite slow-turning wheels of war).
But enough of that! I will not speak of war!
For embryos of future wars more terrible
Than the last are borne over broad backs of sea
And land with each new telling, and in this wise
Are planted fatal seeds in fertile hearts.
Let poets be dumb; let men forget.
Let those who must remember swear by Styx
Henceforth to quiet, that there one day be an end to it.
Let us instead recall Love born of Death
And Darkness; from Love, Light with its companion, Day.

III

They'll say it isn't true: Love born of Death.
They'll tell you only darkness comes from Darkness.
I'll tell you not to argue, save your breath.
Only the heart that fathoms its own darkness
Can witness truth, and by it can be measured
Every word that enters through the ear, that outward
Heart. There are Truth and Wisdom duly treasured;
Evil, falsehood, nonsense quick discarded.
The things I would forget, flesh will remember—
The heat of bodies huddled close still cold
(A trial keeping warm these long years after).
So many dreams, so many stories told.
What use to speak? What use so many words?
Our broken lives? Bright world tumbled, shards.

IV

Her warm breath on my neck, my page her shadow,
She reads, then gently chides me for my scale:
*So dour, so minor. Come, let us walk in the meadow
Of asphodel.* Thus drawn I leave the vale
Of Mnemosyne, and, reentering the world
We did not make or choose but have made home
With our presence and our grieving, I find it good.
There seems no need to speak when she has come
As if, Order and Beauty never born,
Blind Confusion reigned, all chaos, bliss.
Impiety, how one forgets to mourn
The myriad great losses, swept up by this . . .
This *here. Dear one,* she says, her cool hand on my arm,
It's meet that we be joyful; it is no harm.

V

It's meet that we be joyful; have we not heard
The shades singing from farthest Tartarus?—
Burlesques, of course, and lamentations, but also odd
Light airs, such as would sing ones wholly careless.
I nod, for we have heard.
                                    Habit bends
Our slow steps riverward, where we will sit
A while and watch the crossings. Charon grins
At us, lifts a hand in greeting;
We wave back then settle deep in shadow.
The clink of coins, the dip and rise of oars
Have always calmed us, softened our grip on sorrow
So that it slipped from us as unawares
As life has slipped from these quietly rising
On our shore—new stars, dimly shining.

VI

Singly they rise, a few in constellation.
She walks among the living; I watch alone
As if, always *as if*, there's consolation
In keeping to the old ways, going on
Despite . . . but no. *Clear your head; start over.*
A long time now the great sky gods are gone.
Exactly what befell them we can't discover.
Murdered, some say; others, *fallen, flown,*
Dishonored in the hearts of men where they
Were but shades, creations not creators.
We bow before the mystery that we three stay.
Though earth be poisoned, the very sky in tatters,
Demeter keeps the harvest; she brings the spring;
I map new stars; command myself to sing.

VII

Silence blooms, astonishing as absence.
I look into their faces long and long
And cannot see a thing. Only presence
Registers—a pressure and a heat along
The lengths of air that they inhabit,
Along my quiet skin which now listens
Hard . . .
            for it knows not what. I sit.
Charon plies his oars. Sweat glistens
On his grizzled brow. *In a god old age*
Is tough and green . . . He can hardly force
A passage through his sorrow for his voice . . .
A geography of scars, of distance, damage . . .
Tomorrow, I tell myself, from the dust I will gather
The mammoth lexicon, the moldering grammar.

VIII

I will make a start tomorrow. Thus resolved,
I close my eyes and let myself be pulled
Over the wide water and down and down.
A sharpness in my mouth, crowding my throat—
Vinegar, clay, absinthe, honey, sorrow.
I'm swaddled in the singing flesh of others.
Rhea's womb, the roiling gut of Cronus.
Blood sings the world a lullaby—
The only world entire. And she is there
Slumbering, deep curled inside Demeter who
Is not Demeter yet, the Separate One
As yet unborn. He will learn to make
Distinctions: child/stone, number, case, and gender;
Deliver us to history from bliss.

III

Turning

A SEQUENCE

Sometimes these cogitations still amaze
The troubled midnight, and the noon's repose.

—T. S. ELIOT, "La Figlia Che Piange"

Breathing

My secrets cry aloud.
I have no need for tongue.
My heart keeps open house,
My doors are widely swung.
—THEODORE ROETHKE, "Open House"

I turn with seasons' turn.
I mourn the loss of light
But love the quiet world,
The trees, diamond'd, pearled.
I pull my wool shawl close.
Threadbare from use, it's cold
Comfort, though it will do
To hide a heart from view
Of wind or stars or cloud
When my secrets cry aloud.

The wind has many eyes.
The wind has sharp, white teeth.
The wind will tell you lies,
Don't listen though she weep.
The stars are gaping maws.
The sky, one hungry lung.
The crowd is just the crowd,
Though it clamor like the sun,
Though it clang like cracked bells rung.
I have no need for tongue.

Day's end: The blinds are drawn;
Dark blankets swaddle sound.
The sky's a board of nails
Upon which silence waits;
Alone, I lift it down
And don it like a dress.

By day, my smooth blue dress,
My rough one, dirty gray;
By night, no blouse but bliss,
My heart keeps open house.

I bid the wind to speak.
I ask the stars to dine.
Pray God to bless the crowd;
Pray God to share this wine.
I let the moon come in.
I sing her madding song;
Our singing births the dawn.
I turn with seasons' turn.
I'm breathed by sky's one lung;
My doors are widely swung.

2 A.M.: The Body as Weaver

The body wants to sleep
Unencumbered by
The bright red yolk of day,
The hungers of its parts,
And the phantom hungers:
Care's bread, the salt of anger,
The name it turns in answer to.

Because the body wants to sleep—
Untouched by light's slow falling,
The pre-dawn house's whispers,
Or its own urges roiling—
And cannot lull the world,
It learns instead to steal,
To weave each thread of sense
       into its dream:

            The bladder aching full
            Become the urgency of sex.
            The smoke-filled room only
                a dream of fire,

Because the body wants to sleep.
And for a while it works.
And then the fiction fails.
And then the body wakes.

Waking

The long day dies; I walked the woods alone;
Beyond the ridge two wood thrush sing as one.
Being delights in being, and in time.
The evening wraps me, steady as a flame.
—THEODORE ROETHKE, "A Walk in Late Summer"

The day barely begun or near its end,
Or meandering around its central pole,
I leave the kitchen, quit the desk, come home
From where I've been, and, sky still looking in,
Curl beneath a quilt and close my eyes.
My hand in sleep curls round the worry stone
You gave when once you called me friend and blessed
My ears with seas of words. Now you haven't
One. The light falls hard, brittle, dry as bone.
The long day dies; I walked the woods alone.

I fill my pockets with what solace can
Be found within my reach on trees or strewn
Amid deep shadows on the ground. Mostly
My fingers close on moss and rocks, leaving
To time the leaves and other beasts with tongue
Enough to watch with me until the moon,
Forsaking Endymion, slowly rises,
Your face scarcely concealed behind her own.
I ask, weep, argue; you don't— . . . Listen!
Beyond the ridge two wood thrush sing as one.

I listen. Around me the darkness moves
In ripples like water's surface broken
By pebbles thrown. In the wake of this new song
The clear reflection wavers and the moon
In this moment is just the moon and I
Am here, without you and alive. I climb

The ridge, walking toward the sound as if
Entering there, I might one day return
To my own spare chambers: ears' roar, heart's thrum,
Where being delights in being, and in time.

Ears' roar, heart's thrum. Close as I dare to come,
Thrush song is what I breathe when I inhale;
Exhaling, I swear, it's helium comes out.
The moon, grown light, rises ever higher,
Pulls the string of my attention tight until,
Hoot owl, tree frog, cricket making their claim,
It breaks like a cloud bursting into rain.
Or a spell. Loving you, I lost the world.
And losing you? I thought I'd lost my home.
Though evening wraps me, steady as a flame.

Three O'Clock

after Elizabeth Bishop's "Song for the Rainy Season"

A flash of light, the rattling pane,
Sleep scurries frightened like a child
At three o'clock, I wake to rain.

My body tenses. Not again!
A simple prayer, pure, undefiled.
A flash of light, the rattling pane.

Day in, day out, it's all the same:
The coolness of the bathroom tile
At three o'clock, waked by rain.

Could such storms bode the final reign
Of the staring rock unmagnetized,
Difference that kills, the shattering pane?

If so, somehow, I must remain
To see bookworm, silverfish, and owl
Inherit this house, waked by rain;

To praise the mildew's growing stain,
Cherished indifference running wild
Through milksoft light, the rattling pane
At three o'clock, I wake to rain.

4 A.M.: Reentering the House of Dreams

And now let us consider the secret life of houses—its rages, its sorrows, its dreams. Let us lie still and listen to its longing. Or, in the midst of machinery's din and mutter, let us turn one ear into a sieve and sift the quiet from the roar, the quiet from the quiet, the house's quiet whisper from its unquiet hush. Begin, rush! to enumerate its dangers, for you cannot exhaust them:

Without nostalgia, each board remembers tree and holds within its heart a hankering for change beyond the seasons' ken. What's more, they understand—and herein lies the danger—what, with luck, they might have been. For years they have listened to the winds' ceaseless tales of travel, the rains' raucous sailing songs. And yet we stand amazed when on gray wet mornings in answer to the river's rising call our houses loose their moorings and set sail. And who wouldn't crave the fluency of snakes, the agile grace of birds—to say nothing of their song? And so, with the patience and ardor of saints, boards dedicate themselves to fire, seeking transcendence through the dark and rising plumes of deadly smoke.

And shall we speak of wires—the sharpness of their tongues, their ceaseless chatter, the anarchic plots they weave the while we sleep? Of locks and doors and the many unclosed eyes? Of walls that long to touch, but shy, cannot come close or even speak? Of glass—its awful calmness? And what that one day brings? And who dares linger over pipes, or long contemplate their tears?

Better to build one's house upon the sand, a stone's throw from the sea's throat. Better still to be the hermit crab who does not build at all.

Turning

Whoever has no house now, will never have one.
Whoever is alone will stay alone,
Will sit, read, write long letters through the evening,
And wander on the boulevards, up and down.

—RAINER MARIA RILKE, "Autumn Day"

The sun is a candle my body must cradle,
Must hold at its center like an unborn child.
In the deepest part of night I will listen
For its pulse, resting my hand at the place it makes
Radiant and warm. And yet when winter turns
I know it is I who will labor to be born,
I who now labor to lure the light inside—
A saucer of milk, a glass of clear blue water
Left on the windowsill. Still the days wane.
Whoever has no house now, will never have one.

And whoever has a house will long to travel,
To leave the well-worn books, the writing table,
The plants that sulk and wither when we fall silent,
The dishes, the clothes that molder for want of touch,
And worse, the thousand objects waiting at
Attention, unearthly still and mute as stone.
If the body can't have light, it wants a body
Warm beside it through the lengthening night.
Pile blankets on the bed, unplug the phone;
Whoever is alone will stay alone.

Chafe as the spirit will there's nothing for it;
No exercise of will will change your life
Or cry a house or lover down from heaven,
As if the in-lit god who gave that staggering
Injunction inexplicably withdrew
Whispering: Rest; now the time has passed for changing.

And so begins your long and dark exile
In the country of yourself just as you are.
There you will marry restlessness and longing,
Will sit, read, write long letters through the evening.

Or else, lost in the foreign landscape, words
Slip through your hands so that night after night
It is the page, the contours of your pen,
Your desk's rough grain that draw you near to them
As they were flames kindled by the angel
Of your touch; yourself become a minor sun.
For three days now a steady rain has fallen.
My body lends its warmth to whatever's near.
I fold the night wind close, the shivering dawn,
And wander on the boulevards, up and down.

6 A.M.: Meditation: Entering the Mind of Winter

The lamppost is cold only to the touch, but lonely often. For who, hastening home of a winter's evening, reaches deep within his pocket not to retrieve the odd dollar or door key, condom or cough drop, lint or loose change, but rather the unsheathed, unadorned hand?

And rarer still, who claps his fellow on the back or grazes the world in passing?

As for me, I hurry home, muttering no small thanks.

Rising

Yes. It is time to go for food.
See how the light brightens in the windows,
See how the wind rises again, air freshens,
Sun, sun come to me here, come here I am.

—HILDA RAZ, "Lacunae"

Letters. One endless letter in my mind.
So much I have to tell you: everything.
All roads—the lengthening light, the robin's song
That wakes me, the motion of wings that stops the heart
(For the first time in my life I want to see!),
Mapplethorpe, myth, biology—no road
This mind strolls down that doesn't lead to you.
To hear your voice, to see your hands touching
Anything . . . your breath, your body's heat: that's good
To me. Hunger. Yes. *It is time to go for food.*

In that other room, angry voices. A loaded
Gun under their bed; you've looked, raising
The heavy mattress, stood too paralyzed
With fear to touch. There's a phone beside
Your bed, though you call no one. It's the only
Home you know. Each nerve waits. The storm blows
Over. Terror settles in to stay. The farther
Away you move the closer destruction comes. Can't sleep.
Knife, Mace, a woman's book tucked under your pillows.
See how the light brightens in the windows.

She knows grief: a close room without windows,
Closed throat, the fetid smell of fear,
A dusty corner where a child is crouching,
Dull and deep boneache from lying in
All day. Landscapes where nothing moves. No rain.
No wind. Sisters bending over their lessons

Late and early, heavy-headed, in different
Rooms, geographies, lifetimes. Meeting.
My Siamese twin, my second heart. Loneliness lessens.
See how the wind rises again, air freshens.

Now, slowly, life unfolds—a crumpled sketch
Culled from the wastepaper basket for
Whatever comes of recklessness and grace,
The ministries of light, a fluent hand.
The body, too, unfolds—sure
In its self-knowledge, fierce in hunger, calm
In the trembling, dazzling, blazing, shattering world.
I fall open, encyclopedic, unabridged;
My every organ sings you like a psalm:
Sun, sun come to me here, come here I am.

Coda

A book for the blank bone-house hours
When time weighs heavy on our hands
And chaff like us is burnt away
By sun or borne aloft on winds.

Long use has left the binding weak;
Disuse has left it brittle.

Either way, it is the same.

⁂

Your hands, once gentle, rifle pages,
Strew cake crumbs, drip coffee stains.
You budget time; you talk of wages;
You leave the book out in the rain.

By your accounts, nothing's changed.

⁂

The binding gives, the pages scatter
(You turn your hands to other plots) . . .
No matter. Leave them to the winds.

The careful crows will cry them up.

EPILOGUE

Chamber Music

I. Faces

She would have sworn summer was the season
    That she loved,
Its lambent light, the length of days in which
    She could fold two
In every one, so that each morning's page
    Or thought would seem
To her, by evening, yesterday's. Sure,
    She'd have qualified—
She hated storms; how suddenly wind could come
    And fell one of two
Loved window-trees, so that where once had been
    A choir of green,
The intimate companions of her days'
    Slow labor,
Now there was only empty sky—blank white,
    Blank blue, blank gray—
And down below, for weeks, that awful stump.

Still, sun-drunk and dazzled by blue sky,
    By the sheer gift of
The illusion of time and time to spare,
    She'd soon forget
The gripe of fear-gripped bowels, storm-shattered nerves,

And that's when she would swear that summer was
    The season of her soul's
Expanding. But she knew what summer was,
    Or else
She learned, when new resolves, new friends, fresh hopes,
    New loves had come
Sudden as bloom or summer storm and left
    Before the leaves
Had donned their death masks.

II. The Weighing

After the one who'd brought the music back
     had died, the music stayed.
The other one who'd taken everything
     when she had gone—music,
Words, the sun—, returned, brought nothing back
     that anyone could name,
Took nothing further away . . .

                         She means, the weight,
the wedge of grief remained.

III. Dwelling

Dear God, this dusk
your sky has gone
salmon and slate blue,
and this alone
would be blessedness—
to lie here in the quiet
intent upon a page
I cannot read,

           yes,
this alone
would be blessedness—
not only salmon sky
and this your bluest hour,
but more so, grace
that turns these tired eyes
windowward to search
the common day.

I think that I could live
joyfully in days,
in seasons and in days,
but it's a long walk to freedom
and history's a blood
hound at my heels.

(The river is wide
I can't cross o'er
Neither have I
Wings to fly . . .)

Meanwhile, the future
loads its shiny revolver,
holds cold metal flush
against the temple
of blessedness; the present
shatters:
        fear
              and worry,
hope
    and scurry,
                  plans,
plans, plans, plans, plans;
the gift a burden, a stone
in the belly where breath
and sun had been . . .

⁌ༀⅽ

The day as gift, the day as burden;
Whose wish she woke with: bird's or man's

What could all that matter
After the shattering
(Shuddering)
She imagined?

And it was not the future
She so feared,
Nor was it the past,
But the world that waited

(Rowdy commerce
And loud
Clamoring)—

Crouched, she would have said,
Crouched like some soul— .
Hungry mechanical beast—

Just outside her door,
A beast that would
(Of this she was quite sure),
Were she to rise
And take the staircase down . . .

Long since,
Her eyes have drained
The final dregs
Of color from the sky.

Inside the colors
Warmed her;
Left her calm.

No,
She would not rise,
Would not go down,
But would remain

In the house of light,
Where birds chitter
And sing each morning,
Their passionate wish
Her wish.

IV. Spring

homage to Thoreau
and for Robin Becker

I

Because the breaking up of ice on New England's ponds
still moves the great sloth heart of Henry Thoreau
in reciprocal motion, intricate and large

Because it is March and shirt-sleeve weather

Because each winter takes its toll, and light
has traveled long to reach us here

Because inner space is vaster

II

Because a presence rises like a star
exploding the field of vision

Because these women adjust the blinds to
blot out the sun, to save
the eyes from glare

III

For the ear there is no such protection

Because the voice is a scalpel that clean
ly opens the heart

IV

Because a palm laid firmly on a knee
in casual conversation
approximates the heft and heat of sun

Because *even ice begins with delicate crystal leaves* . . .

The feathers and wings of birds
still drier and thinner leaves

V

Because once again nature scribbles her poems
leaves them everywhere:

the lungs, the lids of roses, the lobes
of ears, their farther reaches,
the fingertips, the palms, the lips, the tongues

VI

of women

VII

Because, though it is cold again,
passing kindness lingers, warms

V. Morning Song

The world sleeps snug in its glistening white shell.
You'd never know it held a core of fire,
A sliver of the sun, fine needle of
Bright bone, stitching up the fabric of a life.

Before the day is sewn familiar hunger
Wakes her. Perhaps she stirs inside a nest
Of wools and flannels, cheeps once and softly
Begins to sing, and hunger forgotten, sleeps.

Next, the shovel's slow caress against
The crust of snow, snow's soft sough of resistance,
The rhythm of Paul's work, his steaming body . . .

Before she sleeps again she blesses Paul;
This austere tenderness is all she asks.